I AM BUT A STRANGER HERE,

HEAVEN IS MY HOME

Kathy,
Mary God always
watch over you and
your loved ones.
12-13-18.
Mary Rita Waldschmidt Bauck

MARY RITA WALDSCHMIDT BAUCK

Version: 032318

Cover Art by Erin Kathleen Connell
Author Photo by Laurie Bauck Connell

I Am But a Stranger Here, Heaven Is My Home
Copyright © 2013-2018 by Mary Rita Waldschmidt Bauck
Published by Lulu.com

I am but a Stranger Here, Heaven is My Home / Mary
Rita Waldschmidt Bauck

ISBN 978-1-300-81543-3

God Angels Spiritual Suffering Hope Peace Jesus Christ
Holy Spirit Ghost Christian Love

Printed in the United States of America

This book is dedicated to

My family and friends.

God has blessed me abundantly

For this I am truly grateful

ACKNOWLEDGEMENTS

THANKS to my sister and best friend, Geralyn Waldschmidt. To my writing practicum instructor Ami Hendrickson, a well known author, for the immense help she has given me. To my friends in our writing class especially Janie, Paula and Lisa and others who have been so helpful.

A SPECIAL THANKS to Bob Ghent, an author who has helped me out a lot with this book. I had loads of questions and he had the answers and was very patient with me.

THANKS to my wonderful daughter, Laurie and my two special granddaughters, Erin and Kelsey Connell for their help with the cover and putting the book all together.

MOST IMPORTANTLY IS THANKS TO MY GOD for all of His inspiration, hope, love, and guidance.

TABLE OF CONTENTS

FRIENDS ARE LIFE'S GREATEST TREASURES
I am wealthy beyond all measure,
My treasures are mounted high.
They reach towards the heavens
As they stack up to the sky.

I'm truly blessed for having riches
That far surpasses any gold,
And they can't be bought in any store
And never will be sold.

My treasures build a stairway
And on them you can depend.
God's name for the greatest treasures
It's simple - He calls them "FRIENDS."

He has blessed my meager existence
With something that can't be taken away--
Something I can always count on
Day after beautiful day.

When I'm not feeling quite up to par -
My friends will always pray
They always bring joy and laughter
And sunshine to my day.

Oh, you could search the wide world over,
But nothing could compare
To the love that flows from friends -
The warmth is everywhere.

And so when my prayers are daily said,
A special prayer I pray,
"God bless my friends, take care of them,
Each and every day."

AND THE DAY CAME WHEN GOD TOOK HIM HOME

I wrote this poem for a dear friend who died several years ago. His name is Doc. He was in his 80's and died from cancer.

He was in charge of St. Vincent de Paul Society at our parish and over the years helped hundreds of people. The poor would come knocking on his door and he would take good care of them.

He was blind but if you didn't know it, you wouldn't realize it.

I was the parish secretary at the time and Doc and his wife would walk to church every morning and would stop by my office to say hello, see how I was doing, or just tell me they loved me and appreciated all the work I did for the parish.

Doc was kind and generous and never had an unkind word for anyone. He is deeply missed.

The poem I wrote about him is probably what happened when he got to heaven.

AND THE DAY CAME WHEN GOD TOOK HIM HOME

And the day came when God took him home...

God welcomed Doc with open arms and said, "I'm very pleased with you my son. Welcome home at last. I've waited a long time for you. You served me well and now what I promised has come to pass,"

The doors opened wide to the Kingdom of God, the angels in Heaven rejoiced. The trumpets sounded, music filled the air and now Doc had to make a choice. For God showed him the mansions he could pick from, a new home in Heaven to reside. God showed him the best because Doc served him the best, but Doc, being Doc called God aside. He said to God, "I appreciate your offer and I know I shouldn't refuse, but something much smaller, much planner would suit me just fine," and God was certainly amused. Doc saw God reflecting in silence, but old habits are hard to break. "Give the mansions to those more needy – please for my sake."

And the day came when God took him home...

God smiled at Doc and said, "Very well" and they walked and searched a bit. Then there at the end of the garden was a small house and Doc said, "Now that should fit."

So he settled in and was happy and pleased. He worked in his garden all day. He laughed and he smiled as he looked all around and watched the children at play.

It was so good to see again and what a sight to see – the beautiful flowers, the birds in the air, the grass as green as it could be. And the visitors that came to the door were quite different than those that came before... There was Mary and Joseph, Paul and John – what a sight to lay his eyes on!

What a day it was when God took him home...

Now he smiles down on us below and his prayers you

*know we all have. And as happy as he is there, I know he
wouldn't want us to be sad. We learned a lot while he was
here – How to pray and be kind to others. The best tribute
we can pay him is to continue to be kind to our brothers.*

*And so Doc we bid you adieu, we certainly will miss you
dear friend. Take care and God bless and pray for us until
we meet again.*

And the day came when God took him home...

DEAR LORD JESUS

Dear Lord Jesus,
Help me on the path of life.
    The road is long and the journey rough.
I don't always make the right choices -
    I try Lord – you know I try.

Forgive me when I open my big mouth
    And stick my foot in it,
Or say or do something that you wouldn't be pleased with.
    All I can say is, "forgive me Lord – I'll try again."

I know I'm not perfect and I can finally accept that.
    I have always strived for perfection
But know it is out of my reach --
    I'm only human, Lord.
    This too took a long time to accept,
But I am learning to accept --
    I sometimes wish others could accept it.
        And not keep pointing out my mistakes.

I love you Lord –
 I love you so much I feel sometimes
  I will explode with my love for you.

I trust you Lord as I have not trusted another.
 Even when I have had illness, intense pain, suffering,
  And the pain of losing my brother when he was only
twenty four and in the prime of his life.
The pain of watching my parents suffer and slowly die.
 It hurt Lord – it hurt real bad.
But I never turned away from you –
 How could I?

I know you know what is best for me,
 And during the really rough times
I imagine your loving arms wrapped around me –
 Holding me –
  Caring for me –
   Consoling me,
    And always, always loving me.

You dry my tears and you help me
 Find the joy in the little things in life –
  The birds, the butterflies, my cats –
All of your creatures and all the beauty that surrounds me –
 From the most beautiful sunset
  To the shattering thunderstorms –
Your presence is always there.

I thank you for the many friends
 And loved ones you have given me.
  And I thank you for giving me life –
   A loving heart and soul –
    Compassion –
     But mostly for my love for you –

You are so good to me!

Even if I fail to tell you I love you,
Please always remember I do.
Your Faithful Servant,
Mary

SOMEONE

I was lonely, but no one cared,
I was troubled and they were aware,
I needed someone to talk to,
Someone to share the pain.
But everywhere I went it was all the same,
They had no time for me.

They wonder why the world is so bad
With crimes galore – it's oh so sad.
"Someone should do something" they say,
They talk about what should be done night and day,
But they forget they are "Someone."

And if each "Someone" would do their part
And give to someone else a little of their heart,
A little of their time, their love, their care,
It would make troubles a little less rare,
And maybe in time love would abound,
And "Peace on Earth" could be found,
Won't you be that "Someone?"

HOME IN THE HOUSE OF THE LORD

The first priest I worked for was a good priest. I only worked for him for a little over a year as he got cancer. He was in the hospital and I would make the sixty mile round trip every day to let him know what was going on in the parish and to see if he had any instructions.

After he was in the hospital for about a week, the Bishop of our Diocese came and told me my boss had cancer but I was not able to tell anyone. This was hard knowing and not being able to tell anyone about it. After the priest was released from the hospital, he told the parish. His health failed rapidly.

I took care of the parish plus I took care of him. It finally got to be too much for me, so I had a lady come in and take care of him during the day, and a man came in at night.

Once, as I left work a song came to me and I got in my car and wrote as fast as I could. It is called, "Home in the House of the Lord." The following is the song:

"Home In the House of the Lord"

The doctors told me I was going to die
And that would make most people cry.
But I am thankful and glad to say
I'm on my way to the house of the Lord.
I'm on my way to the house of the Lord.

The people have been praying for many a day,

Praying for the Lord to send healing my way,
But the Lord said, "I want you,"
And I'm happy to go,
To be home in the house of the Lord.
To be home in the house of the Lord.

Now please don't cry and worry about me,
I'm happy with the Lord and I'm finally free
Of all the pain and suffering cancer brings,
Now I'm home in the house of the Lord.
Yes, I'm home in the house of the Lord.

Heaven is the place where our Savior is at
Peter, Paul, Mark and Matt
Mary and Joseph, they're all here with me,
It's the greatest place to be,
In my home in the house of the Lord,
In my home in the house of the Lord.

When a priest dies, he lies in state in the church. We held a Mass the night before the funeral. Several priests, family, friends and parishioners attended. I played guitar and sang in our music group. We sang the song I wrote for him at that Mass.

After Mass, several people came to the rectory. The family really liked my song and they wanted me to sing it the next day at the funeral Mass. The assistant to the Bishop said that we couldn't do it. One priest, some of the family and me were standing in the hallway discussing it. The priest said the Bishop usually runs late and if one member of the family would approach him when he arrived and asked him if we could sing my song, he would probably say yes.

My music group played before Mass and I didn't know if we would be able to do my song or not. Then an usher came up to me and said, "I don't know what it means, Mary, but you have the go ahead."

Then a family member gave me an ok sign so we sang the song at Mass. At the funeral Mass there were a couple of Bishops and several priests that said Mass.

It was a beautiful Mass and I know the deceased pastor was home in the house of the Lord.

THE ROSARY

Fr. Brown was Irish so I made him a rosary out of green ceramic beads. Each bead had a shamrock on it. The beginning of the rosary started with a Celtic cross on it. Father Brown really liked it.

The rectory used to be a convent with four bedrooms. Over the years two of the extra rooms were used for different things. One of the rooms was used for the pastor; the extra bedroom was available in case one was needed for a visiting priest or overnight guest such as family.

At the front of the rectory was my office and Father's office. My office was close to the front door and I was able to watch out the window when someone came. We had bird feeders out there and I enjoyed watching the birds.

There was a long hallway and at the end of the hallway was a large picture of Jesus. Father Brown used to walk up and down the hallway while saying his rosary.

Father was dying of cancer; we kept him at the rectory until the day before he died. He was in a lot of pain, so we took him to the hospital. The family told me he had the rosary I made for him around his neck when he died. The family wanted me to have it back and I would have liked that.

The man who took care of him at nights would use that rosary and prayed it with him every night. After Father Brown died, his caretaker said that he would like to have the rosary as it meant a lot to him.

Father Norm, a close priest friend said he thought Father should be buried with it.

There were three places for the rosary to go. I walked up and down the hall praying the rosary. I looked at the picture of Jesus on the wall; I asked Him, "Jesus, what should I do with the rosary?"

Jesus replied, "You made it for him, Mary. It belongs with him." So Father was buried with it. Everyone had peace with that decision.

Father Norm gave me a rosary that he purchased at the Shrine of Saint Anne duPere in Canada where he and Father Brown would often go. The rosary is larger than most rosaries; it had brown beads. I appreciated the rosary as it was special, because of the connection of two friends and me.

CLOROX, MY LLAMA

My dad died in 1989. In 1994 I bought several llamas. Usually when they got out of their pen, my sister and some of her children would catch them and put them back.

Once I was alone. One of my llamas, Clorox got out. Usually I could hold out a dish of grain to them and they would follow me back into the pen. I tried that and everything else I could think of. Clorox stood still and wouldn't move. Finally I said a prayer to my dad, "Dad, you know how hard it was for you to get your cattle and hogs back in their pen when they got out. Please help me."

The llama moved towards the gate. It was as if someone was behind Clorox and tapping her rear. She went where she was supposed to and then stopped by the gate. I prayed to Dad again and asked him to walk her into her pen. Just like that, Clorox went inside and I closed the gate. If I hadn't seen it with my own eyes, I never would have believed it.

DREAMS

No matter where we are in our journey to the Lord, we need to have dreams and hopes. Keep your dreams alive and some day it will come true. On that day you will be filled with so much joy, you will feel like your heart will burst. Thank God for making all of your dreams come true.

THE WORLD'S BEST SWEETHEART

Valentine's Day is for Sweethearts
And alas, none have I,
But then God reminded me of Him
As He smiled down from the sky.

He said, "I'll always love you,
Upon me you can depend,
I'll always stay close beside you,
I'll always be your friend

For the love I have for you,
On earth none can compare,
You know I'll always be with you,
You know I'll always be there."

So on this day for lovers,
You need not feel alone,
He'll always be close by you,
Waiting to take you home.

And on that glorious day,
He'll wrap you in His arms,
And you'll always be safe with Him
Keeping you from all earthly harm.

GOD, WHERE IS THE SUN?

One Sunday I came home from church and sat in my car. My hands were on the steering wheel and my head between my hands. My body was racked with pain. I have had pain for over twenty years plus numerous other medical problems. I'm wasn't complaining – there are several people who are worse off than I am. I gladly offer up my suffering to God to use where it is needed most.

This morning, however, it seemed as though I couldn't handle it any more. I asked God, "Where is the sun?"

At that moment a large orange cat jumped up on the hood of my car. Then he walked to my open window and came in and sat on my lap. I felt God sent this cat to help me through the hard times. I named him Sunshine.

Over the years Sunshine has helped me immensely. He seems to know when I am having a hard day. He jumps up on my bed and comes under my left arm and cuddles up and I pet him and it helps.

(This is an excerpt from a book that I am writing entitled: Memoirs of the Farmer's Daughter.)

SAINT MICHAEL THE ARCHANGEL

I am a retired parish secretary. I worked for the church for over seventeen years. During that time I served seven priests. When I first started working for priests, I had them up on a pedestal. I thought they could do no wrong. When you sent them a birthday card, it had to be a holy one. I didn't think you should send them a funny one. I learned so much over the years. They are human just like us. They have their faults. As to sending them funny cards, they like that. They have a sense of humor too. They have feelings like all of us. Running a parish is not an easy task. People in the parish don't always agree on everything, and so the pastor has to try to keep everyone satisfied. As we know, though, that can't be done. They do the best they can.

Every time we would get a new pastor, I had to let him know how things had been done in the past. The new pastor would see how the parish was operating, then they made some changes. Most were good but occasionally there were a few that the congregation didn't especially care for.

I liked almost all of the pastors I worked for. Sometimes it was hard making the changes they wanted, but they were the boss and so I had to change. It seemed as though I would just get used to how they wanted things done and then the pastor would be transferred to another parish. That was hard, but on the whole I was able to adapt as necessary. One priest, however, stirred up trouble. I had a difficult time dealing with him, so I prayed extra hard. I prayed to St. Michael the Archangel to help me.

He heard my prayers. The pastor was transferred to another parish and he was replaced by Father Michael. That Sunday we had new missalettes in the pews (these contain prayers and songs). Who should be on the front cover? St. Michael the Archangel. Under his picture it said "defender of justice."

The following week I went to St. Mary of the Woods College to work on my Masters in theology. We had to walk to a shrine that was quite a long walk. I didn't think I would be able to walk that far, but I gave it a try. A nun in a golf cart came up to me and wanted to know if I wanted a ride. I got in and she introduced herself; she said, "My name is Sister Michael."

Saint Michael the Archangel answered my prayers! Father Michael was a wonderful priest and everyone liked him.

The following poem I wrote in 1997 when I was at St. Mary of the Woods College, in St. Mary of the Woods, Indiana.

MY SOUL CRIES OUT

My soul cries out to you, oh Lord,
Hear me and answer me.
I long for your peace – I long for your love.
I am nothing without you.

It seems as though I can't get enough of you,
I am consumed with your love for me –
I am so unworthy Lord.

15

Thank you for showing yourself to me.
Thank you for sharing your life with me –
For being a part of me.

There are others, Lord, who don't know you –
Have never been told about you.
My heart goes out to them as do my prayers
That someone will tell them about you
And your great love.

I need you Lord – please don't ever turn your
Back on me.
Show me, Lord, what you would have me do
To better serve you.

Make me humble Lord,
Grant me peace – grant me patience.
I am forever in your debt.
Thank you Lord.
Your faithful servant,
Mary

"GOTCHA"

When I first started working for the parish, I was a secretary. In those days, the pastors personally asked men to be Eucharistic Ministers, Ushers and Lectors. Women were never asked.

A modern pastor transferred to our parish. He had me type up four different signup sheets that included Mass Servers. He had me put them in the back of the church.

From the time Father Bob told me about what he was going to do until I came to church on Sunday and heard the pastor talk about it to the congregation, I kept hearing a voice in my head saying,"Sign up to be a Eucharistic Minister."   I kept saying to God that I was all ready doing too much for the parish.

After Mass I used to go to the back of church and into the parish hall and talk to people, but I knew if I did it that day, I would end up signing the paper. Instead I walked out the door to the parking lot and smiled to myself and said to God, "You didn't get me this time!"

The next morning Father Bob came into my office and handed me the signup sheet for Eucharistic Ministers. He said, "I don't see your name on here, Mary." And this voice in my head says, "Gotcha!"

Needless to say, I signed the paper.

HE TOOK AWAY MY PAIN

I have lived with pain for over twenty years. I am not complaining, there are people worse off than me.

One year during Lent, I went to Pittsburgh, PA for a weekend conference on Our Lady of Medjugorje. For the conference I stayed at the Burning Bush, a House of Prayer. While there, the pain was excruciating. At the Burning Bush they had a chapel set up in one room where you could go in and pray. It seems like my agony is always worse at that time of the year. I suffer along with Christ.

On an altar in the chapel at the Burning Bush, there was a bust of Jesus. There was a crown of thorns on His head. He had His head held back and looked like He was in so much pain. There were tears of blood coming down His face.

I put my hands on His head. I asked Him, "Jesus, please take away this torment so I can get through this conference on Your Blessed Mother. If you want to give it back to me when I get back home, that's ok, but it is hard to concentrate on the speakers at the conference when I am in so much agony. I want to hear what Our Lady of Medjugorje has been saying while appearing to six young children in Yugoslavia. Please grant me this Lord."

There was warmth in my hands and that warmth went all through my body and went all the way down to my feet and then went out of me.

I thanked Him.

18

For the rest of the conference, I had no pain what so ever. Carrying this cross for so many years, it was almost hard to comprehend that He took my pain away.

After I arrived back to my home in Michigan there was no pain for two days, then the pain came back tenfold. That was ok with me. I offer my pain up to God and tell Him to use it as He best sees fit.

I thank God for all He has done for me, my life, my family, my friends, but most of all, my love for Him.

A LEGION OF ANGELS

Once I was having a Tupperware party at my house. I had invited several ladies and wanted the house to be clean when they arrived. I was working hard but was far from being finished. I didn't know what to do, so I called my mother and asked her if she had any suggestions. She replied, "Pray to the angels and ask for a legion of angels to help you."

I couldn't believe what she said to do. I had been praying to the angels but never thought of asking for a legion of angels to help me.

As soon as I got off of the phone I prayed for a legion of angels and I couldn't believe the results. The house got cleaned so fast and I wasn't working that hard. I was able to sit down with a cup of coffee and relax before anyone arrived

A ROBIN NAMED "MISS KITTY"

On a Thursday, a robin, "Miss Kitty" I called her, came to build her nest on top of the mailbox at the rectory. The wind was blowing all day. As fast as she would bring up bedding for her nest, it would blow away. But she never gave up - she was persistent - just as God is in His love for us. Thursday evening before I left for home she had the bottom layer of her nest done. When I came to work Friday morning, she had it half done.

All day Friday she toiled. She would take her long beak and dig in the ground and bring up dirt to pack in her nest to make it more secure. Then she would take her belly and chest and pack it all down tight, going around and around in a circle to form a secure nest. It reminds me of the story in the Bible about building a strong foundation for a home.

Miss Kitty has taught me perseverance - no matter how hard the road gets and things look desolate, never give up - all things are possible with God.

I put a sign on the mail box, "Maternity Ward" and asked the mailman to put all the mail in the box below the mailbox.

Soon Miss Kitty had a nest she could be proud of. Then she disappeared. I finally called the Nature Center. They said a robin builds her nest and then lays one egg a day until her "clutch" of four or five eggs is laid. Miss Kitty was gone for a week, with no sign of her. Then much to my surprise, she came back around 1:00 p.m. and sat on her nest. I was thrilled! The Nature Center said since she wasn't there all week, she must have gotten hit by a car and died, but here on Holy Thursday she returned.

I thought about her persistence in not giving up. On my way back from getting llama feed that day, I saw an old man by the side of the road raking stones out of the grass. I saw a lot of people doing that, but what was different about the old man was that he was in a wheel chair. Too often we get caught up in our problems and say, "Oh, poor, poor me" instead of thanking God for what we have.

As the new leaves on the trees and the daffodils, crocus and other spring flowers come to life, there is just a few more days until Easter when our Lord rose from the dead and new life in Christ began.

As I look out my window at the rectory and see her snuggled in her nest, I am reminded of how Christ died for me and rose again. I am so unworthy of His love, but am very thankful. As Miss Kitty sits contentedly awaiting her new arrivals, I sit contentedly awaiting Easter morning.

God's Creations

"There is a time to live and a time to die, a time to mourn and a time to be comforted." A robin made her nest on the mail box at the rectory where I worked. I along with parishioners and children enjoyed looking in her nest and seeing the cute baby robins. When I came to work one morning, I checked on the robin's babies and they were all dead. It was so hard to deal with...I buried them under the pine trees. They were crying for food yesterday but I thought the mother robin would come so I didn't give them anything to eat. I don't know what happened to her - perhaps she got hit by a car, perhaps someone in their zeal

21

to see the babies touched the birds in the nest, perhaps another bird came to the nest - it is hard to say. I keep saying, *"I should have given them some worms, or I should have done...,"* it is like when you lose a loved one, you say the same things - *"If only I had done things different."* However, we need to remember we are not in charge - it is God almighty and if He wanted things to be different, He would make it so.

When young children and babies die, I feel the reason for this is because God doesn't want just all old people in heaven - He loves children, babies and people of all ages. Perhaps the same is true of all of the creatures He makes. My theory on Heaven is that it will be filled with animals, birds and fish - I can't imagine God making such beautiful living creatures and not have Heaven filled with them.

When you lose a loved one, you need to keep in mind the good memories of that person and how blessed you were to have them for a time, and so it was with the robin and her family - it really was a beautiful experience. I can't even begin to tell you the joy I had of looking out the window by my desk as I worked.

God has made such a beautiful world - we really need to try and appreciate it, pay attention to it and enjoy it. Years ago when my Aunt Harriet, who lived in Milwaukee, Wisconsin would come to the farm, she gave us a new way of viewing the world. She appreciated nature so much. We would go for a walk on the farm and she would stop and pick a flower off of a weed and remark how beautiful it was. When we saw weeds our first thought was to chop them down, we didn't appreciate the beauty in them. She changed our attitudes. She would also stop and look up and marvel at the different types of clouds. She lived in a big city with lots of skyscrapers so I would imagine it was hard to see the clouds. Now, I am always looking at the clouds and all of the other things that God has made. She gave me a new appreciation for them.

Life is too short, take time to stop and look around at all of God's creations - He really made a beautiful world and we should take time to enjoy it.

CALLING ALL ANGELS

Whenever I get in a car, whether I'm driving or someone else is, I pray to God and all of the angels to protect us. I also pray that we won't be the cause of an accident.

My daughter, Laurie, and her family live across the state from me. Whenever I go to see them, Laurie always comes and gets me and drives me home. It takes about three and one half hours to drive one way. I'm just not up to making a trip that far by myself due to my health.

Once they spent the week-end at their boat that is docked about one hundred miles from me. They wanted me to come for a visit for a week. I was really looking forward to that.

Laurie and their boxer, Mollie, came and picked me up. Her husband and their two daughters headed across the state to their home.

It was a beautiful day and as I got in the car, I prayed to God, St. Michael the Archangel, my guardian angels and a legion of angels to get us safely to my daughter home. We were on the highway for about an hour and enjoying our talking. Laurie started to pass the car in front of us. A car in front of them pulled out in front of us. There was no place to go, so we hit the car. A young seventeen year old boy had missed his exit and decided to cross over to the median where the police cars go through. He hadn't looked to see if the road was clear to pass. We hit him hard and I had visions of pieces of metal and glass coming through my body. I'm very thankful it didn't.

My daughter was ok, she had minor internal injuries. She called 911 and then her husband. I'm so glad my granddaughters were with their dad and not with us.

I had braced my feet to the floor as if I was using the brake. I put my hands on the dash for support. All most immediately after the accident happened, a lady came to my side of the car to see how I was. She was a heart cardiologist. She thought I might have broken my leg, but she must have felt the pins in my ankle from an old injury.

While she was checking me out, a policeman got in the back seat of the car and held my head straight. I needed to be brought to the hospital in Lansing. I am overweight and was worried they wouldn't be able to get me out of the car. It was amazing how fast the ambulance got to us. They slid a board under me and managed to get me out and on the stretcher with no problems. I apologized to them for being overweight and was worried they might injure themselves. One of them remarked to my daughter about how I was worried about them. Laurie said, "That's just the way my mom is."

When Laurie first got out of the car, she went to check on the young man whose car we hit. He was out of the car and seemed to be ok, but they took him to the hospital in the ambulance with me. A policeman took her and Mollie to the hospital.

In the meantime, my son-in-law and granddaughters were on their way to the hospital. They said they saw a double rainbow and it seemed to end over the hospital. I felt God had sent one rainbow for my daughter and one for me. As smoothly as everything went, I knew it was God and all the angels watching over us and protecting us.

They checked me over at the hospital and X-rayed me. Nothing was broken but I had badly injured my right leg. They gave me a walker to use when they released me. It hurt so much to walk with it but I was no good on crutches. They told me if I couldn't walk, I would have to stay at the hospital and there was no way I was going to do that.

Curt, Laurie's husband had driven his truck there and they pulled it close to the curb so that it would be a little lower for me to get in. It still was hard to get in.

From there we went to a fast food place to get something to eat. Then we went to where the car was towed so they could get my luggage and things they had in the car. The car was totaled, but because my son-in-law had made sure when they bought the car that it was stronger and held up better in case of an accident. That was proved by us not getting hurt worse.

Laurie and Curt got me a wheelchair the next day and I used it for a long time. I still need it once in awhile but I use the walker most of the time.

I sure am glad that angels are such a part of my life. Without them, my daughter and I might not be alive or in such good health today.

WORKING FOR THE GLORY OF GOD

Once our priest asked the congregation for a volunteer to fill the holes that were on the lawn. A parishioner came with his riding lawn mower and trailer full of dirt and completed the job.

When I type the bulletin I always put a thank you for the work that people do and mention their name.

The bulletin was full, so I was going to put the thank you in the following week. The parishioner that did the work came in my office and was complaining. He said, "The pastor asked from the altar that he wanted a volunteer for this job. I did the job, so I think he should announce from the altar that I was the one who did it."

When he left my office I was inspired to write the following poem:

THE GLORY OF GOD

I said I was working "for the Glory of God"
   As I went about all that needed to be done.
I was a hard worker - that couldn't be denied,
   And I made sure I told everyone.
Goodness knows I did a lot.
   I was President of this and Treasurer of that
And I made sure that no one forgot.

After all, I was working "for the Glory of God"
And I wanted to shout all I did from the top of the steeple,
   But then God came and said to me,
"You're not working for my glory but for the glory
   from the people."

I hung my head in shame, the Lord was right you know,
   Everything I did was all just for show.
I enjoyed getting the pat on the back and
   all the words of praise,
I forgot the Lord himself will reward me in His own way.

If I get all my rewards while I'm still here below
   And shout all my deeds for all to know,
When to the Pearly Gates I arrive
   The Lord will greet me and say,
"There's no sense in coming inside."

"I had so many special rewards for you --
   a party I had planned,
With all the saints and angels we had formed a celestial
   band.
To greet you when you came because you had served me
   so well,

27

But unfortunately you couldn't keep your good deeds to
  yourself but had to tell and tell."

"And so there's no sense in the party -
  nor the treasures I had mounted high,
Because you boasted so much about your good deeds,
  that they echoed across the sky."
"He who humbles himself shall be exalted" -
  "Don't you remember I told everyone?"
"And he who exalts himself shall be humbled -
  so keep quiet when goods are done."

"And so I'll send you back below - you can give it one more
  try,
Continue to do all your good deeds, until the day you die.
Work quietly, work humbly and please don't shout it from
  the steeple,
Remember to work for the Glory of God and not for the
  glory from the people."

MY GUARDIAN ANGELS

Angels have always been a part of my life as long as I
can remember. I was probably four or five when I started
playing with my guardian angels. My brother, Paul, was
four years older than I was and boys have other things they
want to play with. There were only two siblings in our
family at that time.

Most people think they only have one guardian angel,
but I had two or three. When we played together, we liked
to play in our "club house." I would put two chairs side by

side. Then I put a sheet over the chairs and crawled underneath with my guardian angels.

They were the same age as me and they wore the same type of clothes that I wore. They didn't have halos or wings. This was real exciting, talking and playing with them. It made me feel real good.

We had a lot of fun. Sometimes we would have a tea party with my set of play dishes. We talked a lot about the angels in heaven and the martyrs. We talked about what it was like to be an angel. I always wanted to be a saint or a martyr. I wanted to suffer for the Lord. As years went by I didn't think about wanting to do that. God never forgot, I have had a lot of pain and medical problems over the years and I offer my sufferings up to God.

After all of these years, I have tried to lead a holy life, but I have too many faults, so I will probably never be a saint. I believe though that God looks over all of our faults and considers the good intentions we have.

Most people think they have only one guardian angel that watches over them and takes special care of them. I thought that too until about fifteen years ago when I was taking some religious education classes. We had to do a report and the topic I chose was my guardian angels. I stopped and thought about that. I said the plural of angel. It just came out automatically and I started remembering about my playmates when I was a little girl and also as I have traveled through life. It was such a part of me that I never gave it another thought. I had more than one guardian angel and I believe other people do too. It's nice to know that they are always with us.

OUR FATHER

I have had panic attacks for many years. My daughter and I have always been real close. We did everything together. No matter where I went, she was with me until the day she got married.

In the beginning it was hard doing things without her. The first time I took a long trip by myself, it was from Michigan to Pittsburgh, Pennsylvania to a monastery. On the way there I had a major panic attack. I managed to make it to a rest area but didn't think I could make it inside to call for help. I sat in the car for a long time wondering what to do. I thought maybe an ambulance would come and take me to a hospital, but there was no one around to ask for help. Finally I started feeling a little better and managed to go inside and call a priest friend that I was going to see. He said they would be praying for me.

I went back to my car and continued on my way. I was doing a little better, I prayed a lot. With all the prayers and God's help I made it.

I stayed there for a few days and was petrified of the trip home. What if I had another panic attack and caused an accident that injured or killed someone. I was so afraid. I talked to a seminarian who would soon become a priest. He told me to visualize being held in the palm of God's hand. I would be safe there. Then he told me to say the Our Father but not rush through it. He said to meditate on each word and what it meant. I did that on the way home and I wasn't afraid – I was at peace. I made it home safely and in record time. I was so thankful to God for keeping me safe and for His servant who reminded me of the power of God.

THE HOLY SPIRIT

My first year as Director of Religious Education, I was in charge of Confirmation. We had a large class consisting mainly of students from seventh to twelfth grade. Several of our students were in one family; a grandmother, her son, and her grandchildren. We also had a young man with Down Syndrome.

Two days before Confirmation, I visited a chapel at the Gull Lake Retreat Center for a Ministry Formation Retreat. I was on my knees with my eyes closed praying to the Holy Spirit. As I asked Him to watch over our students, I envisioned a dove come towards me. Then I saw doves coming from all different directions. Some had the faces of children – they looked like cherub angels. Others had the face of God. While all this was going on, the tears were flowing from my eyes.

I then asked the Holy Spirit to wrap His loving arms around me and take care of me so that I would do a good job. Then a large dove came towards me with wings spread out and He wrapped His wings around me. It was a powerful experience.

I knew that everything would go smoothly at Confirmation and it did.

I WAS SCARED – GOD GAVE ME PEACE

The year 1975 was a rough one for me. My marriage wasn't that good. I filed for divorce. My nerves were real bad. I was going to group therapy but it wasn't much help. Once on the way there, there were two voices in my head. The one voice said to run the car off the road and into a tree. The other voice said, "No, you have a daughter that needs you."

Thank God I listened to the second voice. When it was my turn to talk, I told the group how I felt. There wasn't much reaction from anyone including the therapist. If I had been the therapist, I would have gotten me help. It seemed like in that group a person could say they killed someone and no one would care. I quit the group and saw my regular doctor and he gave me some antidepressants. They helped a little. While I was at the doctors, he gave me a paps test. The results weren't good. The doctor said I had to be admitted to the hospital and have a D & C and coneazation to confirm that I had cancer.

I was terrified of going to the hospital. My family all lived in another state. I could talk to them on the phone but it wasn't the same as having them near me.

I remember going into the bathroom and standing in front of the sink. I looked at myself in the mirror and asked God, "Why do I have to do this?"

God replied, "Because you have cancer but you don't have to worry, it will all be ok." I felt a calm come over me, I was at peace and I wasn't afraid.

I drove myself to the hospital, had the procedures and a few days later I was released from the hospital and drove myself home. A couple of days later I saw my doctor and was told I had cancer and I needed to have a hysterectomy right away. I was only thirty two and if I met the right man, I might want more children. I went to another doctor and got a second opinion. It was the same as my doctor – an immediate hysterectomy. I went to a third doctor and he said we needed to get a more complete pathology report and ask if the cancer cleared the cone that they took out of me for the biopsy.

The pathologist said the piece they took out of me had not spread to the outside edges. The piece of flesh they took out of me contained all the cancer, so there was no need to have a hysterectomy. In the thirty eight years that have gone by, I have been cancer free. God has protected me and I am truly grateful.

GIVE INTO GOD

Over the years I have told God to use me as He best sees fit. Then when He lets me know what He wants, I say, "That's not exactly what I had in mind."
I have learned that I might as well give in right away because He always gets me.

A Child of God

I am a child of God
And bad tho sometimes I be,
I know the Lord, my God
Will always care for me.

I know to Him I can turn to,
I know on Him I can depend.
I know He always loves me,
And I know He is my friend.

Sometimes when I feel sad,
And things seem to go all wrong,
I turn to God and tell Him
Or sing to Him a song.

And then my heart feels better,
Then I can jump for joy,
I know He knows how I feel
Cause He was once a little boy.

I walk with Jesus and I talk to Him
And we play all day long,
And when I go to bed at night
I say, "Sweet Jesus, I love you."

GROUCHY PEOPLE

I was pleasant, wasn't I?
　　Did you see him smile when I said hi?
I'm so kind and all aglow saying hi to all I know –
Well, not quite all I know – some I try to miss
　　Because of the way they scowl at me and hiss.
From those kinds of people I stay far away,
　　I don't want them ruining my day.
But maybe there is a reason they are always down
　　And maybe there is a reason they wear a frown,
I don't walk in their shoes so I don't know what's on their
mind, all I know is that they are grouchy and unkind.
　　But maybe if I was to smile at them like I smile at you,
Maybe they would change and not be so blue.
　　It's worth a try, but I don't know –
My skin is thin and I get hurt so,
　　But maybe they are hurting inside
And maybe when alone all they do is cry,
　　Something must be wrong or they wouldn't always be
mean,
They must have problems – at least that's what it seems.
　　So maybe I'll try to bring a smile to their face
And maybe the frown they will try to erase.
　　It's worth a try – don't you believe,
It's better to give than to receive?
　　So from now on I'll try to be
Pleasant to all, you can count on me,
　　I'll get brave – I'll take a dare,
And if they scowl I'll just say a little prayer,
　　And maybe God who knows what is wrong
Will try and make these people smile all day long.

MY MOST MEMORABLE CHRISTMAS

My husband and I were in a new town and he was involved in a bad car accident. I found a one room apartment. It was about one and a half miles from the hospital. I used to walk to the hospital every day to see him. I was nine months pregnant and I had to cross a long bridge. It was December and the wind was cold.

Six days after the accident I had our baby girl so I was no longer able to go to the hospital. A friend we had met loaned me their extra car but he forgot to leave me the keys. An elderly lady next door called the police as the car was sticking a little ways by her drive way. The police came to my door and told me to move the car and I explained the situation and said I just had a baby so couldn't push the car. They said not to worry about it as they would move it.

They must have told the lady about me and the new baby as she came to the door with some short bread cookies and a pint of homemade strawberry jam.

Somehow St. Vincent de Paul Society heard about me and came to my door. They looked around and saw that I didn't have a television or a radio. They were all excited as one of them said he knew where they could get me a radio.

I went to the store and when I got home there were all kinds of nice things on the stairs. There was a radio, some baby clothes and some magazines. There also was a dish of homemade cookies and pretzels that had been dipped in white chocolate. I knocked on the door of the apartment down stairs and asked if he knew where the cookies came from. He said he made them. I asked if he wanted the dish back and he said no I could keep it. It was a beautiful glass dish trimmed in gold and it had two handles on it.

The man down stairs took care of his invalid wife and his apartment was nice and clean and then to make all those cookies, I was very impressed.

Here I was in a different state than my family and I felt like the Three Wise Men came. I had nothing except for my new baby daughter and wonderful people who helped me have the most memorable Christmas ever.

This is an excerpt from my book that is in development now titled:

Memoirs of the Farmers Daughter
To check my blog go to:
memoirsfarmersdaughter.blogspot.com

If you would like to contact the author, you may email her at onbutterflywings1212@yahoo.com She would welcome your comments.

Bauck